HOLIDAY DIARIES

OF

FRANK BARTON DAY

1927 · 1928

Two Holiday Diaries
for the years
1927 & 1928

Created by Frank Barton Day
as a 10 and 11 year old boy

A facsimile of the actual pages of the diaries

Fearless Frank Publishing

Published in 2012

Copyright © Michael Day 2012

The moral right of the author has been asserted.

A CIP catalogue record for this book is available from the British Library

Designed by Bill Kocher

Fonts used. Cover - Desdamona; Text - Minion Pro

Printed and bound by CPI Group (UK) Ltd, Croydon, CR0 4YY

ISBN 978-0-9573459-0-4

Fearless Frank Publishing

Tara, Smugglers Lane

Old Bosham

PO18 8QW, UK

info@fearlessfrankpublishing.co.uk
sales@fearlessfrankpublishing.co.uk

CONTENTS

Preface   iii

Introduction   vii

DIARY 1927   1

DIARY 1928   29

FRANK DAY 1917 – 2008
Sitting on the nose of his Spitfire in 1942

These are the holiday diaries of Frank Day in 1927 and 1928, aged 10 and 11,
written and illustrated by him as a holiday project when he was at The Dragon School in Oxford.
They show considerable talent and humour for such a young boy, and illustrate perfectly the adventures
of a child growing up in the years between the First and Second World Wars.

Fifteen years later he was shot down whilst flying a reconnaissance Spitfire over Crete.
He was wounded, but survived. After twenty-four hours in the Mediterranean he was rescued by Italians,
taken to hospital in Heraklion, and two weeks later he was flown to Germany.

Frank spent the rest of the war as a P.O.W. in Stalag Luft III.
He took part in "The Great Escape" in March 1944, and had reached "Piccadilly Circus"
(the first drop-off point in the tunnel) when the escape was discovered.
With the other men still in the tunnel hoping to escape he had to crawl backwards,
to the tunnel entrance, where the German guards were waiting for them.
They were then marched to the "Cooler" for a fortnight on bread and water.

Frank also illustrated his "Wartime Log Book", which will be published shortly.

Holiday Diary
1927

x

HOLIDAY DIARY

The "KINGSLAND"

SKETCH BOOK

SERIES 351

Containing 30 leaves of Drawing
Cartridge Paper.

MADE IN ENGLAND.

In the following sizes :—

| 5 × 3½ | 7 × 5 | 10 × 7 | 14½ × 10 |

REEVES & SONS, LTD.,
ASHWIN ST., DALSTON, LONDON.

FRANK . B . DAY.

age 10 — 5.

July 31st

Daddy and I went to tea with
Grannie.
We walked past Buckingham
palace

One of the Centrys

Aug 1st

It rained all day. I went to the
Chiswick Sports in the afternoon
In the evening we played a game
of Ma Jong

Very damp

3

Packing for the Holidays
Cloths everywhere

Aug 4ᵗʰ

Off to Poole

4

Aug 5th

We went to Sandbanks
for the day.
I saw a battleship.

Aug6th

It rained in the morning
In the afternoon I went out
fishing with Daddy and Uncle
Stanley.
Crabs took most of the bate

Aug 7th

I had a nice bathe in the
morning
In the afternoon I watched
the boats at the Haven

Aug 8th

We bathed in the morning.
Daddy and Mummy went out
fishing in the afternoon and
caught a fish

Aug 9th

It was too cold to bathe
so we went for a moter boat
trip.

Aug 10th

We went to Sandbanks for
the day.
In the afternoon I made a
big sand castle.

Aug 11th

Barbara and David came
to see us

David

Aug 12th

We all went out fishing
and a lot of the bate was
taken by crabs But we caught
13 place and three eels

an EEl

Aug 13th

It was wery cold bathing.
There was a big Alsatian
on the beach.

Alsatian

Aug 14th

It rained all day.

RAIN !!!

Aug 15th

More rain in the morning
In the afternoon we went
for a ride on top of a
tram.

The Conductor

Aug 16th

We went to Studland
for the day.
And saw the Old Harry
Rocks

OLD HARRY ROCKS

Aug 17th

We bathed at Sandbanks in the
morning, and It rvas very cold
But Daddy felt it most.

Daddy

Aug 18th

We went to the sea all
day In the afternoon I went
for a walk with Auntie Dora

Auntie Dora

11

Aug 19th

As it rained all day we did
not do very much.
Uncle Stanley made a salt
for my boat.

Uncle Stanley

Aug 20th

Auntie Ruth came back from
her Holiday at Eastbourne.

Auntie Ruth

Aug 21st

Mrs Pogue and
Uncle Secil came
to tea

Mrs Pogue

Uncle Cecil

Aug 22nd.

We went to Swanage and
walked over the Hills.

I saw a water
rat at the
Heron.

WATER RAT

The Great Globe Swanage   13

Aug 23rd

We went to the sea all day
I helped the fishemen pull in
there net.

one of the fishenmen

Aug 24th + 5th

We went to Sandbanks
both days and bathed.

Near Sand banks.

14

Aug 26th

It was very cold bathing, and to
keep us warm Daddy bought
a water ball.

Aug 27th

We went to Bole Park in the
morning and to Shell Bay in the
afternoon.
We had tea among the heather

The monkey
+ Parrot in
Pole Park.

Aug 28th

We bathed in the morning
And went to Stromboli in the
afternoon

Aug 29th

We went to Studland for
the day.
And had a lovely time.

Stromboli

Studland Bay

16

Aug 30th

We rode to Sand banks
and stayed there
all day.

Aug 31st

We went to Bournemouth
in the morning and to
tea with Uncle Arthour
in the afternoon

Sand banks Road

Uncle Arthour

Sep: 1st

We went for a bike ride in the
morning   Mary Came with us
In the afternoon we went home
to Chiswick.

Mary

Sep: 2nd

Feeling very dull
we went to Kew Gardens

with Pam and took our tea with us

Pam

Sep 3rd

I went shopping with mother
in the morning and out
with Michael after lunch
Daddy had a lot of
work to do

Daddys Half Holiday

Sept 4th

We all went over to tea
with Grannie
Auntie Dorothy was just
off to Scotland.

Auntie Dorothy

19

Sept 5th

I went to the Science
Museum with mother
and saw some lovely models
of airships

Sept 6th

I played tennis
with Hannah

Hannah

Sept 7

We went out with Mrs Luson
and sailed a Kite

Sept 8th

I went by train to
Victoria to stay
with Grannie.

Our Kite

Ticket collecter
at
Victoria

21

Sept 9th

I went out with
Auntie Mary all the
roads near the Museum were up.

Road mender

Sept 10th

We all went to Blackheath
I was very tired when
I went to bed

I was very tired

22

Sept 11th
___

We went to
Kew Gardens

The pond at
Kew
___

Sept 12th
___

We went to Northwood
To visit Mrs Hooper
They have a dog called
Paddy

Paddy
___

23

Sept 13th

It Rained all day

Sept 14th

It Rained all day

Chiswick High Rd
during the rain

Sept 15

We went to the Dentist

The Dentist

Uncle Bert

Sept 16th

Uncle Bert + Auntie Cissie
Came to see us

Sept 17th

We Went to see
Great aunt Temma

Great Aunt Temma

Packing for School

Diary
1928

HOLIDAY DIARY

1928

II-6

F.B. DAY.

Aug 1st

We were very sorry to hear that we
could not go to Haselmere for the first
part of our Holidays as auntie Phil has
got the whooping cough. She has a nice
little dog called Sally

Aug 2nd
In the morning we went for
a bus ride to Acton. In the afternoon
Pam Mrs Luson and Mr Luson came to
tea

Sally

The Bus conductor

Westminster

Aug 3rd
In the morning it rained very hard
and in the afternoon I had a game
of tennis with Hannah

Aug 4th

We went over to Westminster
and had tea with Grannie

Hannah

High Street Level Crossing, Poole.

Aug 6th
We went to the Chiswick Sports

Our view of the sports

Aug 7th

We went down to Poole
Reggie met us at the station

Our luggage

Reggie

37

3725. Floating Bridge, Sandbanks.

Aug 8th

I had my first bathe
    the water was quite warm

The Sea

Aug 9th
We went to
Sandbanks for
    the day —

The Sandbanks Road

The Speed boat

Aug 10
Hannah & I went to call
on auntie Kitty at
Hill crest Road

View from top of Hill

Aug 11

Daddy & I went in a
speed boat Uncle brought
Buster down to the
beach

Buster

41

Sandbanks Pier (Evening).

Entrance to Poole Harbour.

Aug 13

We went to Sandbanks
but it rained

Brownsea Island

Aug 13

We spent the day at Shore Road
With Auntie Maud

At Shore Road

A Japanese picture

44

Aug 14

We went in the Park
it was a dull day

War memorial Poole

Aug 15

We went into Bournemouth + saw the Japanese
drawing pictures

Aug 16

I went on the Lake
in a canoe

The Lake Poole Park

Reggie came to tea

Hannah & Reggie

Aug 17

Lunch & tea at Sandbanks
We snapped a Hydro plane as
it was flying past

near Sandbanks

47

Aug: 18

We went by moter boat
from Poole Quay to the
Haven.

Poole Quay

The Haven

The Quay, Poole.

Aug 19

Uncle Jack took us for
a lovely moter ride through Poole
Ringwood and the new Forest

Rufus Stone. New Forest.　　　　Howard's Series, 302

New Forest

Lynpool, Poole Harbour.

50

Aug 20

All day at the Sea

Daddy + mummie on beach

Aug 21

Rain! rain! rain!

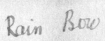

Rain Bow

The Harbour Shore, Sandbanks.

Mr Harvey's Boats

Aug 22

We had another day
with Auntie Maud
at Shore Road

Aug 23

We are going fishing
tomorrow. Daddy has
got a boat from Mr Harvey

The Beach Shore Road

Mr Harvey

53

The Quay & Harbour, Poole.

54

Aug 24

Fished in the harbour
caught 9 doz: Whiting
and 1 cod - David +
Barbara came to Tea

David

Aug 25

We motored to
Bournemouth + saw
The Mikado

The Harbour

The Mikado

55

Dancing Ledge. Swanage.

Aug 26

It rained all day.

Swanage Bay

The Sea at Sandbanks

Aug 27 We went by Motor Boat to Swanage
and walked over the hills to Studland
it was very rough.

Aug 28

At Sandbanks all day
I had a ride on a poney

Aug 29

Mother keeps hiding
Hannah's beret but
H always finds it

Hannah in
her beret

58

Pag 30
At Shore Road
Hannah + my cousins
taken by myself

Aug 31

We played cricket
on the Sands

The Swans had come down
right to the Haven

Auntie Kit took photoes of us all

Hannah Waiting to Bathe.

Sept 1

This ends my diary We are
now packing to go home

_____

64